The NOT-so-WICKED stepparent

I0807605

The NOT-so-WICKED stepparent

Sherrie Mackelprang

CFI
Springville, Utah

ISBN 13: 978-1-59955-301-6

Published by CFI, an imprint of Cedar Fort, Inc., 2373 W. 700 S., Springville, UT 84663
Distributed by Cedar Fort, Inc. www.cedarfort.com

LIBRARY OF CONGRESS CATALOGING-IN-PUBLICATION DATA

Mackelprang, Sherrie, 1975-
The not-so-wicked stepparent / Sherrie Mackelprang.
p. cm.
ISBN 978-1-59955-301-6
1. Stepparents--Family relationships. 2. Parenting. I. Title.
HQ759.92.M23 2009
646.7'8--dc22
2009045585

Cover design by Jen Boss
Cover design © 2010 by Lyle Mortimer
Edited and typeset by Melissa J. Caldwell

Printed in the United States of America

10 9 8 7 6 5 4 3 2 1

Printed on acid-free paper

To Bonnie and Gerry

Praise for *Not-So-Wicked Stepparent*

Stepparents across the country will laugh, cry, and wish they'd read *The Not-so-Wicked Stepparent* sooner! Drawing upon personal experiences, both as a stepchild and a stepparent, Ms. Mackelprang offers tips she calls "power tools" that give blended families concrete advice about effectively building attachment.

I heartily recommend this readable book for stepparents and stepchildren–and anyone else whose life has been touched by the role of stepparenting.

—Corrie Lynne Player, parenting author and speaker, *So Your Teen Knows All the Answers*, *Loving Firmness: Successfully Raising Teenagers Without Losing Your Mind*, and *The Everything Parent's Guide to Raising Your Adopted Child*.

Contents

Foreword

Have you ever played sardines? I'm not referring to the tiny fish snuggled inside of flat tins at the grocery store. I mean the game—the backward game of hide-and-seek. While one person hides, all the other players count with their eyes covered. When the counting ends, the hunt is on. The goal is to find the hidden player and instead of shouting that you've found him, you hide with him. Eventually everyone crams into the same hiding place whether or not there is enough room. It is not a game for the faint of heart. It is an up-close-and-personal game.

Being a stepparent can feel like an ultimate game of sardines. You can run, and you can hide, but you will be found. Any space that was once yours will be occupied with stepparenting undertakings, people, and expectations—all focused on you. You are the star. Former feelings of comfort and certainty will dance in and out of your mind as echoes from the past.

I extend a hand to good stepparents. Having been a stepchild and a stepparent, I know this tour of duty is tough. Raising another person's child leaves a stepparent open for all kinds of criticism. With the criticism, and perhaps less noted, is also the admiration from outside sources, especially those who have been in a stepparent's shoes. I hope to lighten your load by sharing with you the quirky, the odd, the everyday, and some of the challenging stepparenting experiences I've had. I won't give you a list of do's and don'ts, but I'll share the gems of learning that I'm gathering along the way.

One
Ticket to Ride

Where does a family start? It starts with a young man falling in love with a girl—no superior alternative has yet been found.

—Sir Winston Churchill

Standing with friends and family on the day I became a wife, my knees were knocking and my stomach was churning. Sure, everyone experiences wedding jitters, but mine were more like wedding jolts! Not only had I become a wife, but on that day I had also become a stepmother. My husband had three children from a previous marriage—two sons who were eight and five and a daughter who was three.

I entered their family with all the jittery confidence I could muster. After all, I was a schoolteacher. Being able to manage a room full of kids should make me qualified to handle sharing my life with just three. Boy, was I in for a surprise!

Becoming a stepparent is like boldly stepping up and purchasing a ticket for a roller coaster ride. The ride boasts of dropping you farther and taking you faster than any other. You buy the ticket, fully confident of your own capacity to handle the ride. Waiting your turn, you stand heedless of all the screams of the current passengers. Taking your seat, you fasten the five-point safety harness. Up you go, smiling and laughing to yourself as the small locomotive makes its ascent. There is a pause, and a cool silence fills the air as the vessel teeters on the peak of the track. The delicate balance gives way, and the craft takes a plunge over the other side.

You are now hurtling toward an unknown void at a breakneck speed. Screams are futile through your clenched teeth. Flecks of spit hit you on your cheeks as your lips flap open and shut. Knuckles white, you grip the safety bar in front of you. As you hang on for dear life, doubt starts to seep into your mind. Did you make the right decision? Is this really how you thought it would be? Looking right and looking left, the world zips by in a blur. The track is swallowed underneath the vessel, and jumping out is not an option. Just as you are about to succumb to unconsciousness or lose your lunch due to the persuasive g-forces, the track bends, and lights glitter ahead of you. You're going to make it. Maintaining your death grip, you finish the ride. Breathing easier, you're glad to be alive and chide yourself for being scared. Before you roll to a stop and the attendant releases your safety bar, the coaster starts to run its course again. Waving frantically at the attendant, you shout for help. Your cries are drowned out under the rumble of the engine. Finding courage again, you brace yourself for another round.

I had a similar experience on a carnival ride. The carnival used to come to my tiny town each summer. One year, I made up my mind to ride "The Octopus." I had anticipated the ride for weeks before the carnival arrived. I daydreamed about it. I did mock reenactments of it by flinging myself around in circles in my room. The money for my ticket was all saved up. When the carnival finally made it to our town, I was filled with childhood exuberance. After I hounded my older sister, she finally consented to take me to the carnival so I could go on my ride.

Once there, I stared in awe at the blue and white mechanical tentacles of the Octopus. After taking a seat with my sister and her friend, I held on tightly to the safety bar. The ride started slowly. I was doing great. Picking up speed, the gears churned and growled. We spun high and then low, dipping and twirling. My hands strained on the safety bars. My stomach was tossed up to my throat over and over. Suddenly my fondest dream had become a fearsome nightmare. I wanted off! I began to cry. I hollered at the engineer to stop the ride. The noise of the motor drowned my cries. I hung on, shivering, while my sister and her friend just laughed. My teeth rattled in my head as I felt my impending doom. Then, miracle of miracles, the swirling motions slowed, and the ride came to a halt. I still cried, and my sister still laughed. My legs shook as I stepped back onto stable ground. That was my one and only time to brave the Octopus. The experience with the Octopus, though over a brief period, is not so different from the anticipations and ride of a stepparent.

Stepparents are born when family units change. Stepparents come from all walks of life. Some are like me—a single person who fell in love with Tall, Dark, and Handsome, who had children from a previous marriage. Some have children of their own and marry another with children. Whatever the case, blending lives and families is a wild ride of getting to know each other, respecting each other, staying in love, keeping heaven in mind, and keeping your wits.

Cinderella and Hansel and Gretel did little to bring luster to the title of stepmother, or stepparents in general. Both of these tales portray forlorn children who have lost their mothers. Their honorable father remarries and brings into the home a woman devoid of compassion. She is conniving and always searching for ways to bring misery and woe upon her new charges. A slave driver would be more merciful than the wicked stepmother. As a child on my mother's lap, I would shudder at the sad plights of Cinderella and Hansel and Gretel. How dreadful it must be to have a stepmother or even a stepfather. Who would ever wish to have such frightening people enter their life and take control?

The fairy-tale books have now closed, and the true tale of stepparenthood is my life. Since those days on my mother's lap, I have become a stepchild and a stepparent. With no evil motives, I, like so many others, pledged my life and my heart to a family. My plan is to be the not-so-wicked stepmother. Though I may seem wicked at times in the eyes of my stepchildren, I hope in retrospect they will see and understand my love for them.

Naïve is a good word to describe my early insights to stepparenting. Having two stepparents, I thought myself pretty educated for the task. I have observed my stepparents in action, and I figured it couldn't be that hard. Only now, do I understand why my dad and stepdad asked me so many times if I was certain that I wanted to become a stepparent. They had already purchased tickets and tackled the roller coaster. They are still strapped in for the ride. Being wise and caring souls, they both wanted me to be prepared for the huge undertaking of stepparenthood. In my naïve state, I assured them I was ready.

Through my experiences, I have not become the perfect stepparent as I presumed I would. Like the riders in the roller coaster, I have been tossed about in ways I could never have imagined. My arsenal of experiences has taught me that the perfect stepparent is a myth. Similarly, I have found no evidence to prove that wickedness in stepparenthood is inevitable. There is no such thing as a perfect parent in any realm. Parenting is like art. Every artistic endeavor renders a piece that holds beauty for some, interest for a few, and reaps only a shrug from others. The artist has given time and talent to the piece, creating a work to be shared. Yet, creating a piece with universal appeal would prove impossible—just like finding a perfect parent is impossible. The tastes and interests of humankind are so vast and varied that attempting to make a "perfect" painting—one accepted and loved by every person that viewed it—would prove to be a ridiculous venture.

The timeless saying "beauty is in the eye of the beholder" not only applies to art, but transfers to parenting as well. The beauty or esteem of a parent is in the eye of the beholder. We cannot expect to please everyone all the time. We need to behold ourselves and find beauty in doing all we can to be effective stepparents. Parents and stepparents both give energy and talent to the young they are raising. The efforts can be well received, shrugged at, or ignored completely. Like an artist with his work, a good parent or stepparent will have to overcome the efforts that are met with rejection and keep parenting. (A good painter would need to keep painting.) So don't give up the journey. It's always darkest before the dawn, and we've only just begun.

Good stepparenting is a classroom for the stepparent as well as for the stepchild, and personal reflection is the primary text. The ride is unpredictable, but the rewards are worth it. As Helen Keller so wisely put it, "Security is mostly a superstition. It does not exist in nature . . . life is either a daring adventure or nothing."[1] She also said, "We can do anything we want to do if we stick to it long enough." Stepparents, we are living a daring adventure. Let's stick to it.

Note

1. "Helen Keller Quotes," Brainy Quotes, http://www.brainyquote.com/quotes/quotes/h/helenkelle121787.html.

Two

Fairy-Tale Endings

The worst sin toward our fellow creatures is not to hate them; but to be indifferent to them: that's the essence of inhumanity.
—George Bernard Shaw

When did stepparents become wicked? Whose fault is it? As for myself, I blame Cinderella. She really gave us all a bad rap. With her tattered clothes and endless list of household chores, she is the epitome of a heart-wrenching story. If she had only cleaned herself up a little and knocked out her chores a bit more speedily, maybe she wouldn't have made stepparents seem so undesirable. After all, if it wasn't for her bad stepmother, Cinderella never would have met her fairy godmother and danced with the prince at the ball. Technically, it could be argued that Cinderella's happily ever after is a direct result of her stepmother's influence in her life. Could it be that Cinderella's mournful tale was all a setup to knock her stepmother to her knees? Was it just a bad mix of an uneducated girl and a hormonal prince? Well, we'll each have to judge that one for ourselves.

Where did Cinderella's stepmother go wrong? At what point did *wicked* become the dominant adjective for her description? Was it at the point that she said, "I do," and joined her family with another, thus becoming a stepmother? Or was it the point when she decided that Cinderella could do all her bidding and sleep by the fire? What makes step-parenting wicked? Is it the person, or is it the task?

After much thought, I pieced together a few places where the fairy-tale stepparent was placing herself upon the pedestal of wickedness. For starters, the bad stepparent was threatened by the cuteness of her stepchild. She wanted her own kids to be cute. Unfortunately, every fairy tale illustration depicts the stepsisters of Cinderella to be quite unattractive. Instead of working so hard to diminish the cuteness of Cinderella by dressing her in rags and such, perhaps the stepmother should have invested time in her own daughters to help them with their appearances.

Another place where the stepmother went wrong was having Cinderella do all the cooking and cleaning. The girl was learning life skills while the stepmother's own daughters sat around being homely and lazy. This was not the way to build a healthy relationship with Cinderella. She should have fostered a trusting relationship first and worked on culinary skills second. Besides, as Cinderella became more skilled in the kitchen and around the house, she became more of a catch for the prince. This must have added to the stepmother's anxiety, explaining her ongoing crankiness. Plus, the skimpy diet that Cinderella was forced to eat only added to her fairness and the prince's interest in her. This too was a heavy blow for a woman who was so set on seeing one of her own daughters in the royal palace. Ultimately, the stepmother set herself up to fail as she worked so hard to elevate herself and squash Cinderella.

The modern stepparent is not a Cinderella squasher. There are no princes nor palaces to contend for. We contend for higher purposes: peace, comfort, and a level of happily ever after. In order to find it, the fairy-tale ending needs to change. In the end of Cinderella's story, the stepmother was left to live a miserable life as payback for her wrongdoings. Cinderella was granted the happily-ever-after ending, and her stepmother seemed to reap the dreary-ever-after. I vote for a new fairy tale ending. Too many of us are out there working, giving of ourselves, and praying to be good stepparents. Let's repair the unhappy stepparent ending. Let the new ending be, "The stepparent and everyone else lived happily ever after." After all, wickedness is a choice, not a policy.

Three Awakenings

Take care. It is easy to break eggs without making omelettes.

—C. S. Lewis

There is a charming Walt Disney movie called *The Apple Dumpling Gang*. In the film, there is a young boy named Clovis. Clovis is a good boy, but with one fault: Clovis doesn't like to be touched. Whenever someone pats his head or touches his arm, Clovis delivers a swift kick to the shin of the person touching him. Growing up, I was a bit like Clovis. Although I didn't resort to kicking shins, I avoided cheek pinching, head patting, and even hugs. My personal bubble of space was large, and I didn't like it invaded. After reaching adulthood, my personal bubble was temporarily forgotten as I rolled along busy with life.

Amazingly, the first time I sat through church as a step-mother, my bubble returned. This was a twist in my roller coaster ride. Trying to listen to the speaker, my bubble was severely invaded. I had a three-year-old on my lap, manipulating my face like play dough. There was a five-year-old beside me wanting to play doodle games on the back of the program. Beside the five-year-old slumped an eight-year-old who really wasn't sure how I was going to fit into his life. Giving up on listening to the speaker, I gave in to the children's request for my attention. This went on for a moment until the children were no longer in harmony with one another. There just wasn't enough of their new stepmother to go around. Rearranging the kids, I sought to settle them and attempted to rebuild my bubble. It didn't work. My bubble was permanently invaded, and I knew it would remain that way.

I learned quickly that I had to make a choice. The choice wasn't so much about keeping my personal space bubble but keeping my sanity. I had to choose how I was going to keep my happiness when I'd have to give up certain comforts. I thought I was clear on the point of having to sacrifice personal wants and comforts for the good of the family. Prior to marrying, I'd let warm and fuzzy daydreams trickle through my mind of the happy little family we would be. I'd be the model parent, a regular Donna Reed or Carol Brady. Nothing would ruffle my feathers. Ha! My feathers felt ruffled just sitting through church. What had I gotten myself into, and how was I going to make it?

Let me shift gears here for just a moment. My road of stepparenthood had just begun, and I was scared. Determined to succeed, but scared. As I mentioned earlier, there are many different types of stepparenting circumstances. Though each situation is special and unique, I have not known of any stepparenting situation that is easy. Then why do we do it? Why do we take on such a tremendous task? Why do we stare into the face of opposition and sign up for the challenge of a lifetime? The answer is simple and evident: We do it because of love! Love, the driving force behind all that is good. Love, it's the power that took our Savior to the garden of Gethsemane to bleed for us all. This is why we do it. Also, as is stated in "The Family: A Proclamation to the World," "Marriage between a man and a woman is ordained of God. . . . Marriage between a man and woman is essential to His eternal plan."[1] We jump in because we are meant to be joined in family units. In Genesis 2:24 we read, "Therefore shall a man leave his father and his mother, and shall cleave unto his wife: and they shall be one flesh." 1 Corinthians 11:11 repeats the point, "Nevertheless neither is the man without the woman, neither the woman without the man, in the Lord." Our Heavenly Father's children need families. We're not meant to be alone. Though the way is rocky and often tough, love is at the core.

All around the world, people choose how to keep their happiness. It's not just a stepparent thing, but in a stepparent's world it's a big thing. Sitting there in church that Sunday, I needed a solution, and I turned to my husband. I'm sure my naivety shows in telling that I went to my husband over such a trivial matter as personal space, but in a relationship, trivial matters count. My husband and I worked up a plan. We made a decision to sit side-by-side as often as circumstances would allow. The children would then sit on either side of us. He would be my support. My heart was made easy. Sitting beside my husband, I felt secure. A twist in the track was conquered. I was ready for the next one.

Another rude awakening came in the form of barf. Not having children of my own, and having lots of nieces and nephews, I had mastered the art of passing a smelly child back to its parents. I have gagged at the smell of diaper changes and avoided other smelly eruptions. Wondering how parents make it through the stench, I've heard more than one mother testify that it is *different* when the child belongs to you. Somehow, through the bond of parenthood, gross things become tolerable. Regrettably, I now know those parents were right. Assuming full responsibility for my new family, I thought I could handle even the smelly situations. The test came one fall morning, when my stepdaughter opened her bedroom door and heaved her breakfast into the hallway. Taking on a stoic air, I prepared myself for clean-up duty. On my knees, with towel in hand, I made it about five seconds before I was racing to the bathroom to toss my own breakfast into the toilet. Again, I sought the help of my husband. He left work early and came to my rescue. The hallway was cleaned, and I learned that some things are better left to the biological parent.

As a stepparent, I have a valuable role in setting an example and mentoring my stepchildren. I believe what is stated in Proverbs 22:6, "Train up a child in the way he should go: and when he is old, he will not depart from it." Through subtle influences, stepparents help shape and mold their stepchildren, guiding them softly in the way they should go. A biological parent's influence is great. Theirs is the strong voice in a child's life. A stepparent is like the sweet harmony to a biological parent's melody. Yet, there may be times when a stepparent is handed the lead part. As a stepparent I do all I feel I should do to assist in the rearing of my stepchildren, but I understand that the biological parent has a further-reaching influence than I do. Theirs was the first voice in the life of that child. I have to let them have that role. I am often eager to do anything, but like barf, some things are better dealt with by the biological parent.

There is a joy in stepparenting that is beautiful and warm. It enters the heart of the stepparent quietly, like a sweet summer rain. It fills the heart to bursting and leaves it fuller than it was before. In the joyful moments are the memories worth reliving. Tucking the happy memories into a safe place for easy retrieval is a way to keep them fresh.

Among my favorites is the memory of a quiet evening with one of my stepsons. I was still new to the stepparents' world. My stepson was on the telephone, having the kind of conversation that a boy of his young age would. Packing the phone around with him, he was quite animated in his talking. He wandered to where I was and planted himself on my lap. He then announced to the person on the other end, "Don't you know I have a perfectly good mom right here?" His tone was adamant, and though I wasn't the one he was speaking to, his words went straight to my heart.

In sharing these examples, I hope to illustrate a few of my awakenings. First, being a stepparent is tough, but I believe it is worth it and can be a source of sweet joy. Having the support of my husband, friends, and parents has made my ride a little less intimidating. Parenting is not something I could do alone. I hope that every stepparent can have the support they need. Second, I feel there are some things better left for the biological parent. This has been a struggle for me. I too often want to do it all, and my pride is injured when I fail. As much as I would like to have a magic recipe for guaranteed success in every situation, I have yet to find it. However, with faith and love for my spouse, I can keep going and try to be a "perfectly good" stepparent for the children in my home.

As I share portions of my journey with you, I hope you will feel supported. I hope my successes and failures will give you strength and hope to carry on. Let's go for the ride.

Note

1. "The Family: A Proclamation to the World," *Ensign*, Nov. 1995, 102.

Four
The Potato Incident

The trouble with being a parent is that by the time you are experienced you are usually unemployed.
—Author Unknown

In the continual search for my niche as a stepparent, I have often reflected on an experience I provoked as a teenage stepchild. It was fall, and I was in the thick of the quarter's schoolwork. I had a large research paper to write and needed study time to complete it. My mom was still at work, so my stepdad swooped in like an angel of mercy and kindly volunteered to drive me into town and drop me off at the library. After my study time at the library, he would pick me up and deposit me back home. I understood he would be returning to the house twice—once to drop me off after the library and one more time after that. Thrilled, I didn't hesitate when he made one simple request of me in return. My assignment was to scrub and put some potatoes in the oven to bake after his second trip home. That was easy enough. I'd prepped baked potatoes dozens of times for my family.

Wanting to use every spare minute I had to complete my research paper, I made a mental note to put the potatoes in the oven after I saw my stepdad come home for the second time. No problem.

I got quite a shock when he made the awaited second trip to the house. He entered, and to my complete surprise, he was livid. Quickly putting my own work aside, I sprang to do the potatoes. Unfortunately, I had misunderstood what he'd asked of me. I was supposed to have the potatoes baked and ready to eat when he returned for the second time. Oops.

Being tired and in the middle of his busiest time at work, my stepdad didn't mince words in telling me how I'd failed. At this point, we had only been a family for less than a year. We were all still adjusting to some big changes.

I have to explain as well that up to this point in my life, I had never once yelled at an adult. It was an unspoken rule in the world I knew, and breaking that rule meant certain death, or a completely miserable life, void of all freedoms. As my stepdad closed in on me with words about my lack of responsibility and laziness, I bristled. Who was he to question my integrity? He didn't even know me. He wasn't giving me a chance to tell my side of the story. I listened to my stepdad's scolding as long as I could stand it. Then, I charged right in. I hotly defended myself and my actions. I spoke in a volume only previously used on siblings, and I felt no remorse for speaking out in such a way. I was proud of myself for defending my position.

Once my mother arrived home and heard the story, she was shocked and sought me for answers to explain my behavior. I carefully related my side of the story. She instructed me to immediately apologize. I swallowed my pride and did as I was told. My stepdad also apologized to me. In the end, I don't remember who made the potatoes. It was probably my stepdad as I was having a talking-to by my mother, but we did eat potatoes that night. They were a little hard for me to swallow, and I avoided making eye contact with my stepdad throughout dinner. It was a long evening, but fortunately time passed and softened the incident. What seemed like a huge calamity, mellowed to a memory.

Now that I am in my stepdad's shoes, I look back on the Potato Incident with awe. He put up with a lot. I have a new understanding of his side of the story as I too have come home with expectations only to see that they have not been met. The Potato Incident is a source of hope when things don't turn out just right. It serves as a little reminder that life will go on in spite of frustrations. Troubles feel so deep and heavy when we are stuck in them, but hard times will mellow, and we can still enjoy potatoes for dinner.

I gained another gem of knowledge from the Potato Incident for my stepmothering career. Gung ho as I can be, I wanted to help my stepchildren understand the value of work and doing their share. I had just that opportunity when my husband asked the children to complete a task for him. We were building our house at the time, and the kids were to pick up some trash on the side of the house. It was a small mess, one they could manage for their young years. I also had assignments from my husband, and we went to the house to complete our jobs. Our time at the house was brief. Having finished the things I needed to do, I went to see how the kids had done with the trash. To my surprise, the trash was untouched. Puzzled, I quickly gathered it up and threw it away. The kids were very patient and watched eagerly while I did this. Once we were all loaded back in the car, I felt I had to say or do something. Surely I shouldn't let these young people off the hook without some sort of consequence. I flipped through the pages of my mind, searching for instructions on what to do. There weren't any. I knew that disobedience equaled lost privileges—at least it did when I was growing up. It was a technique my parents had used as had the parents of my friends. It should work for me as well. While my insides shook with nervousness, I boldly told the children they would not be able to play with any friends that afternoon. A small riot broke out in the backseat of the car. Tears, moaning, and question after question were sent my way. I didn't know what to do, so I drove in silence for a time. Finding my courage, I dutifully explained why they had lost the privilege. I suppose I thought that my explanation would make them say, "Oh, we're sorry. We'll never disobey a parent again." As you can probably guess, I did not receive that kind of response. All I received was more moaning and grumbling.

That evening, still feeling rattled, I shared the events with my husband. He spoke briefly with the kids and all was well again. I felt like I had a sticker on my head that read, "Rookie." Why wasn't I able to communicate with the kids like he had done? I had to reflect on the Potato Incident to make sense of what I had witnessed. When I dished out the consequence, panic ensued. Yet when my husband spoke and backed up my actions, they took his words with much less resisting. It was similar to me yelling at my stepdad. I had not hesitated to shout at him, but I did not shout at my mom. Let's face it: the relationship between parents and children is different than that of stepchildren and stepparents. Our role as stepparents is no less meaningful—it's just different.

With this unique type of relationship that stepparenting offers, golden moments of bonding and teaching also can happen—moments when we, as stepparents, can impact the child for good. Because of our diverse backgrounds and experience, stepchildren often figure out that there are things we can offer that their parents cannot. For example, when one of my stepsons was in the sixth grade, he was required to put together a science fair project. My husband had limited experience with science fair projects, so I stepped up and volunteered to help my stepson. We worked and put together a fascinating project using soil and electricity. On the day of the science fair, I was fortunate enough to be there. He had a little trouble getting his project to work, and I was honored to help him out. His project did well in the fair, and he went on to the regional competition with it. But more valuable than the award was the time that we spent together in a positive and fun way. Stepparents broaden the horizons of their children by sharing with them new perspectives and ideas.

As a single parent, my husband did the best he could with his sons and daughter. He worked hard and enlisted what help he could. One area where he really tried was in creating cute hairdos for his daughter. He was an expert at creating enough ponytails on her head to keep all of her hair in its place. He would start with two ponytails and keep making more until all of her hair was pulled up. More than once, my stepdaughter was coiffed with four or five ponytails all over her head. She was little and liked her fancy hair. Even to this day she still prefers ponytails to any other styles.

As a new stepparent, one joy of mine was standing in the bathroom styling the fine strands of my stepdaughter's hair. She would stand patiently as I worked a curling iron or blow dryer all over her head. This was something I could offer that my husband could not. She was happy, and I was thrilled. These happy moments are what make it worth it. When my stepdaughter had a dance recital, I felt like all the other attentive mothers. I felt like a "perfectly good mom" as I helped her with her costume and put glittery makeup on her face. Those kinds of moments were what I had envisioned for myself as I looked to my future as a stepparent.

Many negatives can kick us down and unravel the good we can do, and every parent feels some of that. Discouragement is the biggest obstacle that erodes the happiness of a stepparent. It seeps into hair-like cracks and works its way in deeper and deeper, pushing in self-pity and doubt while knocking out courage and faith.

Like Pollyanna in the Walt Disney movie, if we look for the good, we surely will find it. We'll find it in ourselves, our stepfamilies, and in the peaceful moments.

Five

A Hole in the Watermelon

This is the true nature of home—it is the place of Peace; the shelter not only from all injury; but from all terror, doubt, and division.

—John Ruskin

Rumors, gossip, or dirty laundry—no matter the name, a juicy story is a juicy story. These are the kinds of stories that wow or disgust an audience. They're the kinds that will keep a listener's interest as they're spread like jam across bread, getting thicker and stickier all the time. These are the stories that give reason to the line, truth is stranger than fiction. These are also the stories that can create sadness and disharmony. Due to the circumstances of stepparenting, we may encounter many such stories. They're like slices of gooey gossip just waiting to be shared. They may be stories about a former spouse, a stepchild, or any other individual linked to the stepparenting situation. In any case, they are tales where the teller feels superior, and the character in the story is portrayed at his or her worst. Recounting these types of stories may gratify the teller for a moment, but we'd do better to follow the timeless advice from Walt Disney's *Bambi*: "If you can't say something nice, don't say anything at all."

On a golden summer day in sunny, southern Utah, my stepsiblings and I were lounging around the house. Being big teenage kids, we had full run of the house while the adults (my mother and stepfather) were at work. Soaking in our leisure, an unexpected visitor arrived at the door: my stepdad's former spouse. She was giddy and fun. She bubbled through the house making conversation with us all. We all looked on, thinking nothing of her presence. After all, it used to be her house too. I watched her jog down into the basement and pilfer a package of toilet paper. She then did a quick inspection of the kitchen and found a couple more items she needed. Last on her excursion was the refrigerator. Swinging the door wide, she was face-to-face with a half eaten watermelon. Without hesitating, she fished a spoon from a drawer, lifted the plastic wrap, and scooped out the core of the melon. Poking the huge bite into her small mouth, she grinned back at us with her cheeks bulging. I giggled along with the rest of the family. I quite enjoyed her company. This was a fun lady. With the spoon dropped into the sink, and the plastic back on the melon, she closed the refrigerator and disappeared out the door, toting her goods.

I had to leave the house later that afternoon to go to my part-time job. After finishing my shift on that memorable day, I returned home to find the house in a state of near panic. My mother fluttered around ranting about the audacity of "that woman." I knew to whom she referred. Then the inquisitions began. We, the children, were each asked in turn to tell what had transpired that morning. Once the story revealed itself, my stepdad's demeanor changed. My mother continued to rant, but my stepfather moved on. He knew the facts, and that was enough.

As time pressed on, I heard the events of that famous morning retold over the phone to many of my mother's friends and family. I didn't understand all the fuss. So what if "that woman" helped herself to a few things. She must have needed it.

Now that I am in my mother's shoes, I completely understand her frustrations. Having an ex-spouse take the liberty of grocery shopping in my home would rattle some nerves. I think my mother was justified in her feelings. However, I am awed by my stepdad's reaction. Once he understood the facts, he moved on. He did speak privately with his ex-wife, and that was the end of that. I didn't get in on any juicy retellings from him because there weren't any. He is a man that doesn't spread the dirt. If a person hangs his dirty laundry out for the world to see, he is aware of it but doesn't wallow in it.

The point I gain from his example is that pointing fingers at an ex-spouse is a waste of energy. He did the necessary communicating with her, explained his side, and let it go. What a liberating way to function in a challenging role.

In my world, my lips are not often as well trained as my stepdad's. Too often I want to share the juicy stuff that we encounter in our stepfamily life. I have had to train myself to share the juice behind closed doors to private ears. You see, there are times when I think I'd pop if I couldn't vent my feelings. A closed door and a quiet listening ear help prevent my bursting.

Another strategy that I have found useful when the events of our world get too sticky is to take a walk. When something happens that pushes me to pick up the telephone and tell someone about it, a brisk walk around the block settles my emotions back into place. I have taken these walks alone, with my husband, and even with my stepchildren. When the kids come along, I don't tell them the reason for the walk. I let them babble on about whatever and keep the potential gossip to myself. Other times I have taken a pen and scrawled my frustrations out on paper. Then, worried about someone finding my writing, I've thrown it away.

Motivation is another thing to consider when it comes to disclosing the details of our family lives. If sharing thoughts and feelings with someone else will help restore harmony and unity, then go for it. If spilling the details will only bring the kind of satisfaction that comes from shoving a knife in someone's back, then perhaps those things should be kept in private conversations. After all, Miranda rights apply to stepparents, but with a little twist—anything you say can and may be used against you in every situation.

Many times I have gone to my husband, and we have discussed events and challenges at length. I feel the communication between husband and wife on matters that affect the family is vital. As spouses and parents, we need to be on the same page as much as possible. It also helps with the important matter of staying in love. We don't need the whole neighborhood to know what's going on at our house. My opinion on these matters is that only those who need to know should know. Otherwise, the cycle never seems to end. The juicy goop could fill up conversations, spiraling and building upon itself, creating negativity that can block out light can build and unhappiness to ensue. We don't want that.

Share your feelings. Share life's triumphs and challenges. Share them with those who are worthy to listen.

Six

Spirit Prison

Happy will that house be in which the relationships are formed from character.

—Ralph Waldo Emerson

As illustrated by the Potato Incident, biological parents usually get a better response when giving consequences. However, many times my husband is not available to dish out earned consequences, so I am then left to manage the situation. It is a tricky thing to hand out a consequence to another person's child. It can be met with urgent and unpleasant displays of emotion.

In a classroom setting, the rules, rewards, and consequences are taught on the first day of school. A teacher's expectations are made clear from that first day on. The rules and procedures are retaught as often as necessary throughout the school year. Patterns and routines of acceptable behaviors are established and practiced each day in a classroom. Unlike school, my husband and I didn't start our marriage by sitting the children down and reviewing a list of rules and procedures for our life together. It may have been something that would have worked, but we were too busy with settling in to even think of doing such a thing. Once we had settled in and gotten used to one another, it became evident that some household rules would be helpful.

Establishing rules put my husband and me on the same playing field when it came to managing the affairs of the house and children. Once we decided what things were important, we set up some basic rules. Having these common rules eliminated a lot of guesswork. I didn't have to wonder if I was running the house within my husband's expectations or if he was running things within mine. Along with the rules, we worked together on viable consequences that would meet our needs. In my new stepparenting role, it was surprising how setting up rules removed some of the vulnerability that I felt. With rules in place, I was no longer naked. I had reinforcements.

We began with some basic and simple requests, like "respecting one another" and "no friends when the parents are away." Other rules have evolved as the children have grown and needed different structure. For example, when we moved into the teenager stage, we developed a rule about telephone usage and time limits. For me, having structure and unity are like the five-point safety harness on the roller coaster ride. They keep me grounded and safe from flying out of my stepparenting seat. The children know what the expectations are, and they know that my husband and I know them, too. Having unity, as husband and wife, where matters of rules are concerned has also been vital to my stepparenting peace of mind—especially when I am left to enforce the rules.

One of those rule-enforcing occasions fell on me when one of my stepsons was six. Being six years old is an important time. Learning to read, mastering riding a bike, and impressing friends are all big deals when you're six. My second stepson had all these things on his mind and talked about them often. He loves to be social and is a blast to be around. One day the pressure to impress his peers got the better of him. Wanting to show how tough he was, he let fly a stream of swear words on the playground at school. Well, news traveled, as news often does, and made its way back to my husband and me. Grounding was the chosen consequence. Unfortunately, my husband would not be around to supervise during the chosen grounding time. I was on my own. Being nervous, I wanted to be the super-parent. I thought I could cure my stepson of his newly acquired swearing expertise and interest.

His grounding took place on a weekend. I had some painting to do in the house. Just the two of us were at home, and my visions of his dramatic repentance faded as busy reality wrapped around me. I found myself at a loss for words. Busying myself with painting, I chose to wait and let my husband be the one to inspire clean language.

Being young, social, and curious, my stepson parked himself by me and watched as I painted. All manner of things were discussed: dinosaurs, movies, hunting, and more. I figured the little guy was going easy on me. He hadn't shed any tears about having to stay home. Continuing with my project, I was pleased when my stepson announced that he liked being grounded. He explained that it gave him a chance to be at home and talk. With surprise written all over my face, I let him keep talking. He told me that he knew swearing wasn't good and that he figured he'd have to spend some time in spirit prison for his sins. With me choking on a laugh, he proceeded to let me know that he was all right with spending a little time in spirit prison because he knew his dad and grandpa would be there too. My insides roared with laughter at his young insight. I mentally planned a family home evening lesson on the plan of salvation to help clarify his understanding, but my previous anxiety dissolved. He knew where his dad and I stood. He knew he had broken a rule and took the consequence well.

That evening I learned something about success. My ideals let me believe success was having children who didn't make mistakes—silly me. Mistakes are the arena for learning. I learned through my mistaken ideal that my success as a stepparent couldn't be measured by my stepchildren's perfection, but in the quiet conversations we peacefully share.

I wish that every time we had to handle a consequence it went as well as that time with my stepson. Other occasions have really tested my sanity. Yet through them I still find success in the quiet moments and support in unity with my husband.

There was another evening where I spent time with my stepdaughter. I forget what exactly she had done to earn her grounding, but she was young and full of determination. She had decided that her grounding was quite unjust. Certain that she was in the right and my husband and I were in the wrong, she set out to let us know that she was not going to take her consequence without a fight. My husband spoke firm words of counsel to my little stepdaughter. He reaffirmed to her the cause of her grounding and how he expected her to behave. Then, as fate would have it, he left. He had other obligations to fulfill. I was on my own with a very determined child.

My stepdaughter's grounding restricted her from being able to watch television. She had a book she needed to finish reading for school and that was her assignment. As soon as her dad was out of the driveway, my stepdaughter left her room and came and stood in front of me with one hand on her hip. She pointed her gaze at me and said, "Are you going to watch TV?" I explained to her that I wasn't sure. I had some things to do around the house. She then declared, "Well, if you do, you're gonna have to mess with me." At that point my stepparenting mind went blank. I fished for what to do inside my head, but all I could come out with was something like, "You need to go read your book." She stormed around for a few moments then found other interests in her room.

Being at a loss, I made a choice. I felt the negativity in this young girl escalating. I wondered what I could do to brighten her atmosphere. The last thing I wanted was to be locked into a power struggle with her, because I know there are no winners in a power struggle. My decision was to hire a sitter and take myself to a movie. It was all accomplished fairly easily. My stepdaughter is fond of the sitter, and I would not be turning on the TV. I went to a silly comedy and laughed more at myself than the film. Here I was, intimidated by a seven-year-old. I returned from the movie and found things quite peaceful at home. My stepdaughter's cloud of gloom had diminished, and she was quite agreeable. My husband returned and laughed with me. Did I do the right thing? I don't know. All I know is that I did not want a fight; I wanted a peaceful resolution. I was fortunate to have it come about. Since then, my stepdaughter and I have forged through other rough spots, and we have enjoyed dozens of happy conversations. We even make it a point to spend time together when the boys are off hunting or camping. We call it a Girl's Night Out.

Taking myself to a movie was a strategy that I have only used that one time. I feel fortunate that it worked out the way that it did. I'll never know if it was the right thing to do, but it seemed right at the time. With each child being so unique and every situation being different, it is tricky to know how to handle everything that life tosses at us. I find that I send many prayers to heaven. I pray not only for the children, but that my actions won't mess them up too much.

I also have to laugh at myself and the silly events of each day. This doesn't always come naturally. I tend to dive in too deep in each situation, but with a little inspiration and a reminder that I was once that quirky stepkid, I can find the humor. A good hearty laugh can be a soothing fix for a stressed out soul. Humor can remove anxiety and calm troubled waters. Humor works well when viewing stepparenthood in retrospect. How nice it is to laugh through the tears.

Seven
Smashed Sandwiches and Stepdads

There is little less trouble in governing a private family than a whole kingdom.

—Montaigne

Dads have a way of doing things that is all their own. My dad used to make me smashed sandwiches. Once all the fixings were on the bread, he'd smash the sandwich together between his massive calloused hands. He'd then give it to me as a delicacy to be savored and enjoyed. Another specialty of his was the creation of the bread sandwich. He would place a piece of bread between two pieces of bread and smash them all together. I had no trouble eating these interesting treats from my dad, but if my mom had ever tried to give one of these creations to me, I'd have probably squawked a bit. Because the funny food came from Dad, it was cool. Dads have a special way of making the ordinary extraordinary. Stepdads can be cool too. They can inspire and communicate with a panache that cannot be duplicated. They have much to offer to the world of stepparenting.

In my own immediate circle, I am acquainted with several stepdads who are forging ahead with coolness. They are strapped in for the ride and taking its twists and turns as they come. They try to keep an open door and welcome mat out for their stepchildren. In visiting with these stepdads, I was touched by their anxieties. Their stresses were not so different from my own. The obstacles and rewards of raising children are felt and appreciated by every good parent—male or female.

I went to my own stepfather for his wisdom and insights of stepparenting. His stepfathering commitment is large. When he took my mother as his bride, he signed on as the stepparent for seven children. With five children of his own, his fatherly responsibilities now spanned a dozen lives. To his relief, only two of us seven children were still at home when he married our mother, although there were a couple of grown up children that returned from time to time to keep him on his toes.

Accustomed to living in a peaceful suburban neighborhood, the rough ways of his stepchildren took him by surprise more than once. There was one particularly interesting day when one of his new grown-up stepsons returned home from a hike. Flinging his backpack to the floor, the boy swiftly pulled a four-foot-long snake from the bag. My stepdad oohed and aahed at the snake with the rest of us and then recommended it be let loose. My brother wasn't ready to let it go. Instead, he took the snake into the family room to watch some TV with him. True to its nature, the snake wasn't too keen on the television show. It worked its scaly body down between the couch cushions and discovered a tiny gap in the fabric covering. Still holding half of the snake, it took my brother a moment to realize that his pet was slinking away. Jumping up off the couch, my brother tossed the cushions on the floor. The snake had worked itself almost completely down into the framework of the couch.

Tugging at the snake, my brother tried to pull him free. It was no use. The snake was too strong. My stepdad watched with my brother as the last of the snake disappeared into the innards of the couch. My stepdad was floored. He'd anticipated some stepparenting adventures, but a snake in the couch was not one he'd foreseen.

Flustered because he'd already asked this grown boy to turn the snake loose, my stepdad tipped the couch forward hoping the snake would somehow drop out. The bottom of the couch was covered in upholstery fabric, so there were no holes to release the snake. The reptile was in a secure place. With the tension mounting, my stepdad repeated to his stepson the point that he should have released the snake earlier. Poking around, my stepdad located the small hole where the snake had slipped into the framework. Pushing his hand in as far as it would reach, he discovered the impossibility of retrieving the snake through the opening. It was too small and awkward. The opening was tucked too deeply into the corner of the couch. Breathing deeply, my stepdad counted the number of years he had owned that set of furniture. It had been a few, but it had held up well. It had been an expensive set when he'd bought it. Now this grown boy, who had only been living in the house for a short time, had added a new dimension to the furniture—reptilian housing. Tipping the couch forward again, my stepdad's insides groaned. He let my brother slice the bottom of the couch open to retrieve the snake. The plan worked and the snake was removed, but the couch never recovered. It had a yawning hole and dangling fabric for the remaining years of its use.

When I was a young person, my stepdad always seemed so cool and collected, even through the snake adventure. I thought he had it all figured out. He didn't seem to ever have the slightest break in his stride. During the course of our discussion about stepparenting, he enlightened my understanding. Though he held it together, he felt the pressures of stepparenthood as heavily as any parental responsibility. As a stepfather, he wanted to be a positive influence for his stepchildren. There were more than a few golden moments when he was clearly white knuckling the safety bar in front of him.

He recounted another incident to me. Before leaving work one evening to head home, he decided to make a courtesy call to the house to see if there was anything he could pick up in town. He often did this to save on the number of trips we had to make into town and to ease some of my mother's stress as well. That evening my younger sister answered his call. Seeing this as an opportunity, my sister wasted no energy in telling him what we needed from town: Oreos and ice cream. Still being new to the role of stepfather, he was rather obliging. Before coming home, he stopped at the store and bought the items my sister had requested. Entering the house with grocery bags in tow, he was befuddled when my mother questioned him about his choice of purchases. My mother was not one to often buy Oreos and ice cream, let alone at the same time. It didn't take but a moment for my stepdad to piece together what had happened. When my sister had answered the phone and requested junk food, my stepdad had assumed that she was reciting a request from our mother.

Feeling used, my stepdad decided he needed to teach my sister a lesson. He didn't want to be taken advantage of in that way again. After getting a swift scolding from both parents, my sister was assigned to stand by the sink. Taking the Oreos from the package, my stepdad turned on the kitchen sink and ran every cookie down the garbage disposal. My sister watched as all that good junk food went to waste. She was torn because she had not expected him to actually bring home the treats. She thought he would see it as the joke that it was meant to be. For my stepdad the whole incident was a jarring turn in his stepparenting track.

The ice cream and cookies paled in comparison to having dating, teenage stepdaughters. Teenage boys know everything, and the ones that hung around chasing his step-daughters had no humility in telling my stepdad just how much they knew. My stepdad knew that if he ever needed to know something about anything, he could just ask any one of the boys hanging around trying to date his stepdaughters. One such young man triggered a twist in the stepparenting track as he was spouting about making mashed potatoes.

My stepdad was fixing a large batch of mashed potatoes to go with dinner that night. This experience could be named The Potato Incident II or Potatoes Revisited. (My poor stepdad really ought to have other things for dinner besides potatoes. They seem to be more trouble than they're worth.) The kitchen was hot, and he felt like he was the only one working as others looked on. The potatoes were cooked, and my stepdad invested his energy to mash them. Once the creamy white potatoes were ready, my stepdad selected a serving bowl from the cupboard.

The young, self-proclaimed potato guru was sitting on the nearby sofa. He told my stepdad that the bowl he had chosen was too small for the potatoes, and my stepdad should get a different one. Still scooping the potatoes into the bowl, my stepdad chose to ignore the young man. Undaunted, the young man repeated that the bowl was too small and that my stepdad would need a different one. More potatoes made their way into the glass bowl while my stepdad ignored the prattling young man. A third time the young man declared that the bowl was too small. Feeling warm under the collar, my stepdad continued scooping but with more aggression. Picking up the pan, he held it above the bowl. The last of the potatoes came sliding out, dropped into the bowl and flopped onto the kitchen counter. The bowl was indeed too small. An all-knowing voice spoke up from the couch stating that he told my stepdad the bowl was too small.

Fuming, my stepdad turned on the young man. Streams of words shot off my stepdad's tongue like flames from a torch. Stunned, the young know-it-all cowered, broke into tears, and fled to another room. Still steaming with frustration, my stepdad decided to take care of the potatoes. Getting out a larger bowl, he scooped up the potatoes from off the counter and dumped the smaller bowl into the larger one. At this point, the young potato-bowl connoisseur returned to the sofa. My stepdad decided to apologize to the young man for his stepdaughter's sake. The young man apologized for his persistent advice. With the situation resolved, the stepdaughter seemed at ease. Even though the young man had not earned any marks for merit, my stepdad was willing to accept the apology to keep the peace in his home. As he'd wished, after the ordeal, the normal pace of daily routines resumed.

My stepdad invested conscious time and energy into fostering a relationship with each of his stepchildren. For the children who were on their own, he worked to be a friend. For the two of us who were youngest, he wanted to be more than a friend. He understood that we already had friends; we needed leadership and mentoring. He worked to build a parental role with his stepchildren where expectations were clear but fair. He was a parent without being a parent. Leading by example was his most used strategy.

Wanting to create a comfortable bond with his

stepchildren, my stepdad determined that some outdoor activities could provide a nice backdrop for family bonding. Taking some time off, he took his stepdaughters and his own sons to the ski slopes. He'd envisioned a fun-filled day on the slopes, but got a bit of an awakening when it became obvious how much help one of his stepdaughters needed. Wearing borrowed skis and gear, she was having trouble staying vertical and moving forward, even before they all got on the chair lift. That stepdaughter was me.

Everyone dismounted the chair lift easily except me. I tipped right over, and the lift had to be stopped while two ski resort attendants rushed out of their station and put me back on my skis. Wanting to ski, but aware that it would be slow going at first, my stepdad embraced the challenge of teaching this wobbly stepdaughter how to ski. However, I was so busy laughing that the little training he was giving was bouncing right out of my ears. My stepdad modeled and tried to teach me how to angle my skis and snowplow down the bunny hill. With skis parallel and poles waving, I shot off like a runaway train. My stepdad cringed as I nearly took out a class of beginning skiers. All too soon, I wiped out in a cloud of powder, and my stepdad hurried to my side. I lay on the slope, laughing my head off. Anchoring himself, my stepdad wanted to try again to teach his stepdaughter to ski. I stumbled a few times but made it back on my skis. After another lesson on how to snowplow, I shot off like a rocket only to crash again. The zoom-then-crash pattern continued all the way down the bunny hill. Other skiers moved out of my way.

Following patiently, my stepdad met me at the bottom of the hill. I was laughing and talking ninety miles an hour to my sister. At least I was happy. My stepdad invited me to go down the hill again and let him continue to teach me.

I declined, but thanked him. I spent the remainder of the ski trip drinking hot chocolate in the lodge. Scratching his head, my stepdad felt the trip had been a waste. No profound bonding had taken place. What conversations had occurred had been few and limited to the subject of snowplowing. Yet, looking back, he still cracks up at the memory of me careening down the bunny hill. He admits that although the trip didn't go as planned, it has brought laughter to many family gatherings. The trip has evolved into a fun memory in the annals of the family's history. It was time spent together in a positive way, and that is time not wasted.

Not having been there during the formative years of his stepdaughters' upbringing, my stepdad found occasions to worry for our safety and well-being. He knew that there would be times when he would have to take care of business. One night after observing one of his stepdaughters having a lengthy conversation on the front porch with a suitor, he decided enough was enough. She had been out there with this boy until after the sun had gone down. Throwing the front door open, my stepdad chose some choice words and commanded the young man to leave. Obediently he left.

Frustrated and worried, my stepdad struggled to sleep. Questioning his sanity at taking on teenagers, he was grateful for the new day. Wanting his stepdaughter to make wholesome choices, he counseled her on being out late with this boy. The late nights continued in spite of his good wishes, and a short time later this boy became his stepson-in-law. At that point, his paternal worrying dissolved. This was a blessing. The young man that had caused so much worry became a friend. This would-be snag in his stepparenting track turned smooth.

My stepdad learned the ropes of stepfatherhood day by day through life's experiences. He often reminisces on the joyful times too. Christmas parties, Thanksgiving dinners, and spontaneous family get-togethers when the house is full of laughter and conversations are some of the best times. My stepdad also enjoys the attention he receives from his step-children by being invited to take part in the special events of their lives.

My own father is also a stepfather. His role with his stepchildren has been very active. He entered the lives of his stepchildren when they were all but grown. Two daughters remained at home, one of them still in high school. Feeling the instant responsibility that comes with raising children, he stressed and stewed over his youngest stepdaughter's academic performance. Knowing that some things are better left to the biological parent, he chose a backdoor approach to helping her with her education. Being a lover of music, he thought music lessons might lift her up. Making a large investment in a guitar and lessons to go with it, he supported her musical endeavors. Many evenings were passed with her plunking out tunes, and my dad singing along. These were happy times.

Though the script of a stepfather may play out a little differently, his part is equally weighted to, and as challenging as that of a stepmother. A stepfather may feel the pressures of providing food, clothing, and shelter, and he may worry for the spiritual and emotional well-being of his charges.

Despite the knocking about a stepfather can endure on this ride, he can help make a child's life beautiful. Speaking from my own experience, my life has been beautified and blessed by a stepfather's love. Hang in there, stepdads! Your smashed sandwiches can be cool too.

Eight
I'm Not Listening

There is no act, however trivial, but has its train of consequences.

—Samuel Smiles

A mother sat with her children leading them in a family scripture chase. The youngest son was having a tough time paying attention and following along. He found more amusement in teasing his sister than he did in the scripture chase. Frustrated, the mother directed all of her attention to her young son. "Look up Matthew 5:44," she instructed him. He immediately jumped up and scampered out of the living room and into the kitchen. Puzzled, the mother went into the kitchen to find her son. There he was with the telephone book flopped open on the counter. He was quickly running a finger down each of the columns. The mother asked, "What are you doing?" As she moved in closer she could see he was open to the "M" section of the directory. Looking bewildered, the son asked, "What did you say it was again? Matthew what?"

If women are from Venus and men are from Mars, where does that place stepchildren? Do they have their own galaxy? As in the example above, miscommunication among

God's children is not a rare occurrence. I believe stepchildren are hiding under layers of miscommunication. That is their galaxy. They have been programmed by their environment and experiences. We, the brave stepparents, have been programmed by our own experiences. At times, our programs cross and create a mess of static and feedback. Other times, it all seems to click into place. Can we tune in to their frequency? Can we reach into their heads and understand why they say the things they say and do the things they do?

Frequently, I am stymied as I endeavor to comprehend the logic and rationale behind the words and actions of my stepchildren. After digging around a bit, I have found others that feel the same way. To me, communicating with a stepchild can sometimes be like trying to understand the meaning of a new word without seeing or hearing it used in context. It is similar to thinking you understand the lyrics to the song on the radio, only to find out later that what you heard and what was played were two different things. I recently had this experience. I was singing the line, "to the rhythm of the ceiling fan," only to find out the actual words are "to the rhythm of a steel drum band." Personally I like the imagery of the ceiling fan, but a ceiling fan is a long ways off from a steel drum band. Maybe I should try playing my ceiling fan. In any case, eventually—and sometimes with a lot help—I'll get it. Because I wasn't there when the new word was created or when the songwriter wrote the song, I have to use the knowledge and experience that I have to make meaning.

Nurturing stepchildren can throw a few ceiling fans into our steel drum bands. I think it is because I wasn't there during the early years; I don't always comprehend the context of what they are saying, or worse, I'll assume I know the context only to find out later how far off I was.

Another stepparent shared the following experience with me. I feel it illustrates the commonality of step parental struggles with communication and comprehension. It was early in the morning and a busy time for the blended family. Everyone was getting ready for the day and the house buzzed with activity. There was no time to be wasted. Everyone had to do his or her part and be prompt and efficient. This stepparent walked past the open bathroom door to see a stepdaughter standing in front of a sink full of water. She was scooping the water to her face and splashing it all over the mirror and onto the counter. Frustrated and bewildered, the stepparent entered the bathroom and gave the girl a scolding. To emphasize the point and call attention to the mess that was being created, the stepparent slapped a hand down into the sink full of water. Water shot out of the sink and splashed right up into the stepdaughter's face. When the inquisition occurred, the stepdad discovered the stepdaughter was simply washing her face.

Still frazzled, the stepparent waited in the family's Suburban for his daughter and the offending stepdaughter, so the stepparent could deliver them to school. However, the communication frequencies were still muddled. The stepdaughter was rushing to get into the Suburban and barrel rolled over the middle seat and flopped onto the back seat. The stepparent snarled. The girl had not entered the car in a respectable manner. The stepparent felt the stepdaughter was purposefully trying to damage property. Wanting to teach a life lesson and instill a measure of respect, the stepparent made the young girl get completely out of the vehicle and reenter. This time, she was to enter slowly, fold down the middle seat, and carefully settle herself in the backseat. After seating herself properly, the stepdaughter declared that she had only done what she had witnessed others doing.

As in this example, communication between stepchildren and stepparents can be similar to communicating across cultural differences. The stepchild was behaving in a way that she believed to be acceptable—it was acceptable in the first family she knew. The stepparent saw the child as behaving in ways that were contradictory to his way of doing things. They both acted in accordance with their own belief system. The stepparent did not react to the biological daughter in the same ways as the stepdaughter. With the biological daughter, the playing field was different. She was the home team, and in a sense the stepdaughter was the visiting team. They had each gained their early understanding and experience from different coaches.

As stepparents, we often feel we are in the role of training another coach's player. The game is the same, but the hand signals, gestures, plays, and other forms of communication are different. So what can be done to fix the crossed wires? I'm sure that, as in any relationship, valuing the person and the relationship over the circumstance helps untangle the crossed wires. Forgiveness of others—and of ourselves—must be a key, but I confess that when I am stuck in a miscommunication rut, I don't instantly bring this good advice to mind. Humor is an antidote to erode the severity of tricky situations. It may not be prompt in arriving, but I hope with time, all stepparents can look back and laugh the rough stuff smooth.

Assuring me that I am not alone in misunderstanding my stepkids, my stepdad related an experience he survived. My mother was not around, and my stepdad was forced to take matters into his own hands. My sister had done something that concerned him. As time has faded the memory, he doesn't remember her offense, only her reaction. They stood face-to-face, while he lectured her on rules of propriety. Apparently the lecture was drifting in one ear and out the other, because she jumped up on tiptoe and bonked my stepdad on the forehead with her own forehead. She then snarled, "You make me so mad!" Stupefied, my stepdad didn't know what to do. He immediately ended the lecture that had seemed so important, and he made a mental note to keep a larger distance, and perhaps a helmet, between himself and my sister if another lecture ever came up.

Dinnertime is wonderful for family communication. Sometimes the communication leaves me speechless. One quiet evening, we had settled ourselves around the table for dinner. After the blessing on the food, I said, "Dive in." Now, I have to insert something here. At the time, my oldest stepson was on the city's junior swim team. Swim team kept us busy five nights a week and, at times, was rather expensive. So after I invited the family to "dive in," my oldest stepson blurted out, "I need a snorkel." Instantly my thoughts went to swimming and the dollar figure attached to it. I started in on how if he wanted a snorkel, he would have to save up his money. Besides, he didn't need one for the swim team. Looking at me as though I had just stepped off of the mother ship, my stepson shook his head. He informed me that he didn't really need a snorkel. It was a joke. It was to help him "dive" into his dinner.

If I'd had a dunce hat, I would have put it on and sat on a stool in the corner. Why was it so hard to understand the meaning behind the words? I grew up in a family of pranksters. I knew how to joke and be funny. Yet, because I wasn't there from day one with my stepson, I took his words the only way I knew how—literally and at face value. Feeling a little foolish, I finished my dinner and pondered why I had so easily misunderstood him. I could only chalk it up to the same phenomenon that occurs between newlyweds. After the courting period, a couple assumes they know one another. Yet fifty years down the road they are still getting to know each other. How convenient it would be to pop open the minds of our stepchildren and pour in a thick wad of our own interpretations of life. Then we could also pop open our own minds and pour in a similar serum of our stepchild's perspective on things.

Communication barriers surface even when intentions are heartfelt. Living out in the country without the distractions of city life, my dad had some opportunities to communicate with one of my stepsisters. She was nearing the age of being able to strike out on her own. Being older and more experienced, my dad attempted to share some of his wisdom with her. She had recently discovered flirting and men. He counseled her on things to look for when choosing a guy, certain practical things that a girl should look for in a man. He called them rules, which included things like the guy needs to have a job so he could support a family; he needs a car in today's busy world; and he also should have a place to live. Now a man didn't have to measure up to all of these rules, but he did need to have an eye on his future. This was all recited to my stepsister. She took the "rules" and gave them the value she felt they deserved—she found a guy that fulfilled all her dreams, but, to my father's chagrin, the only worldly thing this man possessed was a chicken. He supposed she had not heeded the rules.

Snorkels, chickens, and bonks on the head—all proof that we as stepparents are giving it our best shot despite the illusion that our stepchildren seem to be from another galaxy at times. It is hard when you feel something inside of you and you want to inspire or enlighten your stepchild. It stings when that effort seems to mean so little or go unnoticed, but let's not be "wicked" because of the sting. May we each take up a steam-venting hobby instead—kickboxing sounds nice.

Nine
I Get That When You're Dead

I am absolutely unshaken in my faith that God created us, loves us, and wants us not only to be good but to be happy."

—Archibald Rutledge

I've always had an interest in old things. My mother used to have an old-fashioned, gold colored, vinyl purse. In the purse she kept old items of interest—treasured mementos of the past. There were pairs of elegant gloves from her college days, antique jewelry, a few interesting rocks that her children had given her, and a few old coins. As children we had a reverence for the contents of the gold purse. The purse was usually tucked deep in my mother's closet where it would sit forgotten until one of us begged to have her open it for our gazing. To me, it was a veritable treasure chest that ignited my own yearning for old treasures of my own.

One afternoon my stepchildren and I were browsing through a local thrift store. My eye caught hold of an antique looking bracelet nestled neatly in a display case among glass plates and odd shaped bottles. My curiosity was piqued. Craning my neck, I found the price sticker and was delighted to discover the bracelet was only $2.00. I spoke briefly with the sales clerk, and she took the interesting bracelet from the case and placed it in my hand. It was costume jewelry, but unique to anything I owned. Slipping the silver colored metal around my wrist, I enjoyed the weight and feel of the heavy white enameled flower on the front. In the center of the heavy flower were a couple of glinting rhinestones. Some rhinestones were obviously missing, but it was no less pretty to me. I showed my stepdaughter my find, but she was less than interested. She was busy perusing the aisles, seeking her own treasures. I purchased the bracelet and thought little of it until I decided to wear it on a Sunday.

As I came down the hall dressed for church with the bracelet on my arm, the white flower caught my stepdaughter's eye. She asked, "Where did you get that?" I reminded her about our trip to the thrift store. She announced, "I get that when you're dead." Her statement was as matter-of-fact as telling someone that a storm was coming. Amused but a little stunned, I stood rather like a stump, uncertain of what I should say. After a brief pause, I stated the obvious, "Yep, you do." Delighted, my stepdaughter bounded away. Scratching my head, I wondered if I should be worried about my stepchildren plotting my demise. *Should I have my food checked for poison before I eat it? Should I check for poisonous frogs under the covers of the bed? Nah, I'll just let her dream of the day it will belong to her. Maybe I could put it in a gold colored purse for later enjoyment.*

Thanks to her statement, I was struck with a thought. Children are the heirs of their parents. Children inherit what their parents leave them. My stepdaughter obviously understood this principle of things being passed on from one generation to another. Could it be that in her albeit selfish statement, she was letting me truly share a part of her family tree? Was she accepting me as a parent, not merely a stepparent—or at least she would once I was dead? I'll take it as a yes!

Another experience that left me thinking happened while I was having my car serviced. My stepdaughter was with me, and I felt we were at a positive point in our relationship and that my stepdaughter was really maturing. She was beginning to show that she understood the value of making choices and why I tried so hard to help her make good ones. One area where I felt she was really making progress was in understanding modesty. She could pick out modest clothing all by herself. She was also being choosier about the shows she wanted to see and letting me know if a particular program was inappropriate.

We entered the waiting room of the service station. A small TV set in the room was turned on. Immediately my parenting radar was put on alert. On the television there was a scantily clad woman resting on a bed while a man brought in a tray of drinks. Making a fast judgment about the program based on what I saw, I punched the off button. As soon as the screen turned black, my stepdaughter moaned and said, "I know that show! I saw it at my friend's." Her face was lined with disappointment because it had been turned off. She told me the title, and my eyebrows went up a notch. It definitely wasn't a family program. I wondered where I had failed. How could she believe such programming was acceptable?

Are there lessons that we will better understand after we're dead and have shuffled on to a higher realm? Some things seem to require a lifetime of learning to figure them out. When one of my stepsons was having trouble maintaining friendships, I thought it might be just one of his life lessons and that learning how to help him out must be one of mine.

We took our family to a neighbor's home for a barbecue. There was a lot of laughter, conversation, and of course good food to eat. The neighbors had a son nearly the same age as this particular stepson. The two boys had played together on several occasions. While we were all gathered around the table enjoying our meal, the neighbor's son mentioned what a sore loser my stepson was. The boy continued explaining without any prompting from me. He spoke in flat tones as he shared the story: he and my stepson had been playing a favorite computer game earlier in the week. While they were playing, my stepson had declared, "If you don't let me win, I'm going to leave." Well, the neighbor boy told me that he didn't let my stepson win, and my stepson had left without saying a word.

I was impressed with the frankness of the young neighbor boy. I don't know that I would have had the courage to talk so easily with my neighbors at such a young age. I passed the information to my husband. My husband then chatted with my stepson about being a friend.

It appeared the talk must have had some impact because it wasn't long after that my stepson struck up a friendship with a different boy in the neighborhood. To make the things easier, I'll call this new friend Sam. My stepson spent a great deal of time at Sam's home. I imagined them playing and having all sorts of fun. My stepson was being such a good friend. Then, one evening, Sam wandered over to our house all alone. I was surprised because my stepson was still at Sam's house. Sam asked if he could play with my other stepson. I asked Sam what my oldest stepson was doing at his house. Sam explained that my stepson had come over and immediately gotten onto Sam's computer and wouldn't get off. Sam said that even when he had asked and suggested other things to do, my stepson insisted on playing on the computer. Apparently Sam had given up on my older stepson. Sam had completed chores, run errands with his mom, and watched TV while my stepson was still on the computer. Finally getting bored with my older stepson, Sam had decided to play with the younger one. I was thankful for Sam's honesty. I could tell that Sam was a patient boy, as were his parents. I had no idea that this was how my stepson was spending his playtime. I called my stepson home. Again, he sat through a talk with his dad.

I had zero experience in helping this child to have better friendship skills. After getting his talking to, it was up to me to manage things at home while my husband was away at work. I decided to let all the playing take place at our home. My stepson didn't react. He was content to be at home without friends. Worried about his social life, I invited some friends over for him. The kids all played outside, giggling and having fun, except my oldest. I encouraged him to go outside and join the others. He told me no thanks. He said he was "an inside kind of guy." To force him to interact with others, I fed them lunch outside. That helped him mingle, and he played a little.

Now this stepson is much older, and he is still an inside kind of guy. He prefers a book or his guitar to just about anything. With the passing of time, he has grown into a nice young man. I can see that friendships mean a lot to him now. He has come a long way since the days of the computer game fascination. So maybe we don't have to wait until we're dead to figure some things out.

Tempers can jostle the stepparent track. With my younger stepson, there were times I thought his temper would be the death of me. I must confess that in the moment his outbursts were comical, but the black cloud hovering over him was nearly unbearable.

One Saturday morning, my younger stepson was pedaling his bike home from a sleepover party. The party was at the end of our block, a short distance away, and he had insisted on riding his bike. He had managed balancing his sleeping bag while riding to the house with no trouble. The return trip was less successful. While pedaling, his sleeping bag proceeded to unroll and spread out on the road. Flustered, my stepson got off his bike and let loose on his sleeping bag. He gave it a stern talking to and a few good swift kicks. Wadding up his bag and walking his bike, he made it home, where he let his bag know how crummy it was all over again.

Another example was when my stepson was putting away his folded laundry. He was having some trouble with one of his drawers, which was already quite full. He was working and working to get all he could to fit into it. Pushing and shoving, he tried to close the packed drawer. Each time he would push it closed, something would pop out. Stuffing whatever it was back into the drawer, he'd try again. His determination was impressive, but then something snapped inside him. He began giving the drawer a lecture on its shoddy performance. He punched his clothes and kicked the drawer. With some help, he simmered down, and all the clothes were rearranged to fit into the drawer.

In this case, maybe we'll both better understand the frustrations of life when we're dead.

Bracelets, service stations, computers, and hot tempers allowed me time to reflect. I stretched my thoughts to wonder if my perplexity is a little of what our Father in Heaven must feel about each of us. I can imagine him scratching his head over the thoughts and choices of his earthly children. Perhaps that is the bigger picture we should each tuck into our step-parenting wallets—the eternal plan of happiness. There is a place in it for each of us. We are made better by our service to our fellow man or fellow stepchildren. If eternity is our goal, then we'd better remind ourselves of its glory and say, "I get that when I'm dead." It gives purpose to the twists in the track. Through experience and choices, the tough and the strange can fortify the stepparent's soul.

Ten

Got Bait?

Dear Lord, make me a better parent. Teach me to understand my children, to listen patiently to what they have to say, and to answer all their questions kindly. Keep me from interrupting them, talking back to them, and contradicting them as I would have them to be to me.

—Gary Cleveland Myers

No fish would purposefully gulp down a barbed hook. The threatening hook has to be beautified and made desirable. It needs bait. Obviously we don't fish for stepchildren, nor do we disguise fishhooks for them (at least you better not). However, I have found that I often expect certain behaviors and give certain responsibilities to my stepchildren. The behaviors and responsibilities are often closely linked together. For example, the children have the responsibility of completing their schoolwork. To attend to this responsibility, they need initiative and desire—behaviors. These are like hooks. In my stepparenting fantasies, my stepchildren are bursting with self-motivated initiative and a strong desire to achieve. Reality is a little different. There is plenty of initiative and desire for things like eating a bowl of ice cream, watching a fun movie, or meeting with friends. Desirable activities do not require any bait. The undesirable task and behaviors sometimes need a little bait.

Upon becoming a stepchild, I was frozen with fear to join my new family, live in a new town, and leave all things familiar. I was a small town bumpkin. My new stepfamily was high society in my eyes. How could I fit into their world? I was nearly consumed with anxiety. I was a teenager halfway through my high school years. I had attended school with the same kids since kindergarten. The thought of moving to a new life was not a welcome idea. Though I did little to resist the inevitable changes, my parents must have noticed my hesitancy. They threw me some bait: theater tickets to a local college production. My parents must have known the strategy would work. I was currently on the drama team at my school. I was hooked. The bait was too much to resist. To attend the play, I had to join my family and move into my stepfather's house. It worked. The reluctant daughter was reluctant no more.

Flying down the stepparenting track, I have not been above employing the use of bait. Is it the right thing to do? You'll have to be the judge of that.

In a classroom setting, bait is called incentive. A teacher offers various incentives for a job well done. Extra recess, free time, an art project, or even a class game—these are all examples of possible motivators. In my stepparenting world, I found incentives that work for us, ones we can honestly fulfill. It would be a dangerous thing to hold out a prize and then withhold it once the task or behavior was achieved.

My stepfather also knows that a little bait can work wonders. Feeling the grind of having a house full of kids, my stepdad devised a plan to motivate his charges into action. He had to make the prize desirable enough to ignite the motivation of not only his stepchildren but also his own children. It also had to be something he was honestly able to fulfill. After much thought and budgeting, he decided on the bait: Disneyland. The catch? Each person had to earn their way there. With so many things needing to be done around the house, my stepdad used earning our way to Disneyland as a way to make all the kids accountable for their chores. To keep track of who had earned what, my stepdad came up with Disney-Bucks. Disney-Bucks were the monetary system for earning our way to the theme park. My younger sister volunteered to design the bucks. She drew a lovely caricature of my stepdad in the center with large number ones in each corner. My stepdad copied and cut out a plethora of the Disney-Bucks and held on to them until they were earned. The agreement was that whatever we earned in Disney-Bucks he would later trade us for the actual dollar amount. With money hanging over our heads, the race was on to complete our chores. My stepdad had obtained the desired result. Each of us kids earned Disney-Bucks. My younger sister earned the most. When the time for our trip arrived, my stepdad was true to his word and drained his wallet, paying each child in cash.

My stepchildren are pretty smart and creative. They are good at figuring things out. Like I mentioned earlier, my oldest stepson had a huge fascination with a certain computer game that belonged to a neighbor. You could say he had caught a sort of computer plague. Being a quick thinker, my stepson worked out his own incentive for doing a chore he really didn't enjoy: taking out the kitchen garbage. Trusting as we were, my husband and I didn't notice how it took a while for the boy to complete this chore. I figured he was outside, twirling his bow staff. My husband thought he was just behaving like a kid and dawdling. Come to find out, the boy was actually racing to toss the garbage bag into the trash, run across the yard, ring the neighbor's doorbell, and advance a level on the computer game before returning home. The computer game, though unknown to us, was a huge motivation for him to take out the trash.

Let me jog back to a story I shared at the beginning of the book: my husband had asked the children to pick up some trash. Now, let's suppose that I added to his request by saying something like: "Once the trash is picked up, we'll all have a Popsicle." Would it have changed the outcome? I don't know, but on paper it looks like a little incentive might have eased my mind. I don't pull out the incentives for every situation, but when all else seems to fail, a little incentive or bait can go a long way. Even the great plan of our Creator has a prize at the end if we'll just do our part.

For me, giving incentives helps me feel successful as a stepparent. Incentives help relieve the stress I feel when I have to motivate one of my stepchildren to perform certain chores or obligations. On the side of the fridge we have three narrow slips of paper taped in a row. Each slip of paper has a child's name on it. These are bank accounts we keep with the children. In our house money is a big motivator. Monetary incentives are often offered to the children to inspire them in their schoolwork and daily chores. When life is busy or, thanks to direct deposits, no cash is available, the earnings of the children are written on their account slip on the side of the fridge. No surprise that the children have a keen awareness of just how much money they have earned. When we go shopping and they find an item they just can't live without, we make the purchase, and they subtract it from their account. So when my stepparenting plate is full and the kitchen sink is too, I can call out a dollar amount that I'm willing to pay. Miraculously, the dishes will disappear. The dollar amount is added on the side of the fridge, the child is happy, and my workload is lessened.

Because I teach, I am always concerned with my stepchildren's performance in school. As they have gotten older and the curriculum has gotten harder, we have set a standard payment amount for grades. When the kids earn a 3.5 or higher grade point average, we give them twenty-five dollars. If they earn a 4.0, they receive fifty dollars. This works for us. It has been effective. One of my stepsons had trouble with turning in assignments. He would do the work and then not give it to his teacher. Once he understood he could make some money his grades improved. This boy has even proudly brought home a 4.0. As a stepmom, I don't have to nag about grades. The children know what is at stake. I can leave the nagging to the biological parents.

Another item that has helped me feel successful being a stepparent is a simple chore rotation chart. Chores are a necessary part of daily living to keep a home running smoothly. Chores also help foster responsibility and a sense of satisfaction in a job well done. Chores prepare children for the day when they will have a place of their own to look after. Every time I get to issue reminders about daily chores, I see the reflection of Cinderella's wicked stepmother in my children's eyes. They hate being reminded to do their chores, especially by me. My solution was to fasten to the fridge (the fridge is a hub of activity at our house) a simple chore chart. Breaking down the daily chores into three basic tasks, each child is given a task for the week. The kids rotate chores every week. I wish I could say that this simple chart, made out of paper and paperclips, ended the need to remind the kids about their chores. I wish I could say they all rush home after school to complete their assigned task with enthusiasm, but I would be lying. It has, however, simplified the reminding. Instead of hearing me drone out reminders for several little tasks, they are reminded about one larger task.

Also, by having the chore assignments where they all can see, they often remind each other.

One of the twists in the stepparenting track is that we usually have to work harder than a biological parent would. When a child comes into a home with responsible caring parents, he falls in love with, trusts, and depends upon his parents. A stepparent earns trust and respect. My father could tell me to do the dishes, and I would have obeyed out of respect. My stepfather figured out the value of bait. He would ask me to do the dishes and slip me a Disney-Buck from time to time for my efforts.

I still tell my stepchildren to do things. Many times they respond just fine. When the tension seems tight, I throw out a little bait. It seems to help them respond to their not-so-wicked stepmother a little better.

Eleven
Help!

Children are travelers newly arrived in a strange country of which they know nothing.

—John Locke

Like doing the splits without stretching, stepparenting realities can come quickly and painfully. There is an analogy that I have often heard repeated. It compares a human life to a house. The house is quaint enough, but it is due for some improvements. God steps in to facilitate the improvements. Suddenly, the house is being bumped about in painful ways. Walls are removed, new wings are added, and a new roof is constructed. The remodeling mess is enormous. The little house wonders if it will ever recover. Then the project is completed. The quaint little house is now a glorious mansion.[1]

A stepparent can experience a great deal of being knocked about—much like the little house. I know I have felt like my walls were crumbling down and my foundation was being rattled. I have felt stretched, torn, and broken. Yet, somehow through it all, I have survived and even grown a little in knowledge and understanding. Am I on my way to becoming a mansion?

Teddy Roosevelt once said:

> It's not the critic who counts. . . . It's not the man who points out how the strong man stumbled. . . . Credit belongs to the man who really was in the arena, his face marred by dust, sweat and blood, who strives valiantly, who errs to come short and short again, because there is no effort without error and shortcoming. It is the man who actually strives to do the deeds, who knows the great enthusiasm and knows the great devotion, who spends himself on a worthy cause, who, at best knows in the end the triumph of great achievement. And who, at worst, if he fails, at least fails while daring greatly, so that his place shall never be with those cold and cruel souls who know neither victory nor defeat.[2]

A stepparent dares greatly. A good stepparent understands what it is like to be in life's arena with dust and tears as the medallions of the task. Stepparents understand serving for the joy and satisfaction of doing something good for someone else. Stepparents get to put themselves and their needs last for the greater good of the family. Isn't that what our Heavenly Father would have us do? As we serve our fellow stepchildren, we are serving our God. Then, maybe we too can become the mansions he would have us be.

A good friend of mine has also been a champion in the stepparenting arena. Her stepchildren are grown now, but even the mention of her stepparenting days brings tears to her eyes. Wishing me the best in my endeavors, she repeated to me the words, "Stepparenting is hard. Stepparenting is hard." Those of us in the arena understand the weight and truth of her words.

I can sincerely say I didn't know it would be so hard. With my educator background, I thought I was ready for anything. One thing I could have never prepared for is that stepparenting can hurt so much.

I recently received a note that was penned by one of my stepchildren. It was addressed to their dad, but my husband shared it with me. In doing so, he assured me that I had his complete support and not to worry. The contents of the letter instantly put me into a state of worry. In the letter this child essentially proclaimed that every bad thing that had ever happened to him was because of me, the stepmother. The letter said that I was not liked, and his dad should put me in my place more often.

Upon completing the letter, I mustered enough courage to tell myself, "Big deal." As I tried to go to sleep after reading it, I faced the fact that it was a big deal. I felt sick. I tried to think of what awful sins I had committed against this child. No one thing came to mind, but I mulled and stewed over it for the remainder of the night. I was worried and hurt. I felt like I had been punched in the gut. When daylight dawned, it was all I could do to go through the motions. I wanted to sit in a corner, cry, and lick my wounds. The day wore on and proved to be a long one. I consoled myself with prayer and believing life would go on. I hoped that I would look back on the incident as a badge of courage—a sort of proof that I could make it through whatever trials I faced. I prayed it would dissolve to a mellow memory like the Potato Incident.

Thankfully, the young conscience of my stepchild was pricked. I was given a tear-filled apology. The little person explained that the fault was not mine. I had been used as a dumping ground for blame. My stepchild needed a place to lay all the anxiety and stress of starting a new school year. I accepted the apology and thanked my stepchild for it. It was an unexpected and welcome relief to the tense situation. The heartfelt apology helped to restore my faith in the child, which was something I didn't want to lose.

Valuing the wisdom of one of my stepparent friends, I

related to her a watered-down version of what my experience had been with that letter. I described some of my feelings and the sincerity of my stepchild's confession. With tears brimming in her eyes, she looked at me and told me not to worry. She brought to my attention a simple truth: my stepchild is building character. For this young person to fix a wrong choice showed real developing character. Something was going right in this young person's life. This young person was also working on becoming a mansion.

The more she talked, the more comfort I felt. Perhaps I could look for the lessons in the tough times—my own as well as my stepchildren's—instead of only focusing on feeling the wind being knocked out of my sails. I'm not a saint, and I know that my supercharged stepparenting sails will more than likely be crumpled again. Will I instantly shout, "Hurray! We're all building character!"? I doubt it. More than likely I'll start out with a stoic air. I'll tell myself I can handle it. Then I'll get mad and keep it to myself. I'll smile, but my smile will be tainted with a subtle sneer. Next, I'll probably feel hurt and cry when I think no one is watching. Then I'll share my feelings with my husband or a close friend. By the time I feel better, the problem will have resolved itself, and I'll wonder why it seemed like such a big deal at the time. After the tumult has passed, I'll recharge my sails and stare down the next fiery dragon that crawls in my way. When the next challenge comes along, I hope to roll up my sleeves and say, "I've already dealt with your kind. Go ahead and give me what you've got."

My stepfather remembers a dragon that climbed in his way. He was registering me for school. Because I'd taken the bait to move into his house, school was next on the agenda. Patiently waiting for the school counselor, my stepdad was sure the registration process would be quick and easy. When it was our turn to meet with the counselor, my stepdad got a little surprise. I had some makeup work to do. I had failed a class back in my freshman year. It was an algebra class, and the credit would have to be made up. The dragon wasn't so much the grade or the credit, but the fact that his new stepdaughter had managed to keep her failed class a secret for over a year. My stepdad asked the counselor what the options were for making up a class. There was only one option that was going to work, and he knew it would be a burden on him. He would be driving me to night school in a neighboring town. My stepdad didn't grumble. He quietly took care of transporting me and all the other kids in the neighborhood that were in the same boat. I wish that I could be so forbearing. Through my stepdad's example and actions, my character was strengthened. Years later, I came across a song that summed up my appreciation for my stepfather's part in raising me. I gave him a CD with the song one year for Christmas. My mother told me about the impact of my little gift. She said that he wept to know that something he did affected my life for good and was touched because I recognized it.

A stepmother on the road to changing the image of stepparents related her challenges and outcomes of raising a certain stepdaughter. This stepdaughter tested every scrap of patience the stepmother could paste together. Dishonesty, backstabbing, and substance abuse were all on this young girl's plate. She was on a path of self-destruction, and this stepmother was at the end of her rope to help the girl. Angry words were exchanged on several occasions. Talking escalated to screaming. The stepmother sought her husband's advice and counsel, but, united as they were, the trials continued.

The stepmother didn't give up. She spent time on her knees praying for this troubled daughter. Both parents prayed for a happy outcome. The problems didn't instantly disappear. Things seemed to get worse. The daughter had destructive relationships and stole things. After much struggle, the girl moved out of her father's house. The stepmother and the father were able to maintain only minimal contact with the girl. Efforts were still made to help her find a better kind of happiness. Thousands of prayers were sent to heaven. Over several years, the girl's heart began to soften. Her life found stability. She married a good man and bought a house. Her countenance changed from bitter to peaceful. The relationship between this daughter and the stepmother changed from a very tense and strained one to a wholesome one. "When she was a kid, I never thought I'd be able to love that child. Now she flutters around like a butterfly—so pleasant to be around," the stepmother declared.

This stepmother shared words of wisdom valuable to all stepparents. She said, "Sometimes you just have to back away and let them figure it out for themselves. Life has a way of letting us figure things out sooner or later."

So, stepparents of the new generation, can we face the yucky and hope for the best? Can we tell ourselves, "If it doesn't matter in the long run, get over it?" We may do it through clenched teeth at times, but I believe we can do it. We can be the champions of character building and perseverance (especially when it feels like it's our character that's doing the building). May we bond together and be strong together.

Notes

1. C. S. Lewis, *Mere Christianity,* New York: HarperCollins, 2001 166.

2. Teddy Roosevelt, "The Man in the Arena," Speech at the Sorbonne, Paris, France, April 23, 1910, http://www.theodore-roosevelt.com/trsorbonnespeech.html

Twelve
Power Tools!

All I have seen teaches me to trust the Creator for all I have not seen.

—Ralph Waldo Emerson

I was given my first real power tool about five years ago. It is a nifty staple gun. (I know there are some of you out there who have bigger power tools, but we all have to start somewhere.) My staple gun is school bus yellow and electric. All I have to do is plug it in, and I am ready for business. I can install bat after bat of insulation. Watch me go. I like the way I feel with my stapler in my hand: like a real contractor, slinging my staple gun around. I've become protective of the little gun too. A person's need has to be great before I'll hand over my power tool. When I do hand it over, I get a promise from the borrowers that they'll treat it with care. My little gun has saved me time and headaches. It gets me wondering about other power tools that might make me look cool and work fast. Perhaps I should get a table saw . . .

In my power tool search, I have found one that works for both stepfathers and stepmothers. Have you used it? It's prayer. It's perfect to cut my labor time and help get the job done, especially if I am at the end of my rope and need an understanding friend. Prayer is the perfect tool. It is portable, affordable, and it doesn't care who you are or what the situation requires. It doesn't care if I've brushed my teeth or combed my hair. It always works. Sometimes it works so well, I don't even recognize that it has done its job until I take some time to look back and see.

Several years ago, my stepson went on a field trip with his class. The trip was extensive, and the children were expected to arrive back at the school around five o'clock in the afternoon. Everything was going according to plan, and I had no reason to worry. I went to work and busied myself with the day's demands. As I worked in my classroom, I repeatedly felt the need to pray for my stepson. Puzzled, I rattled off quick prayers in my head and forgot about it. That afternoon, my husband and I parked our car alongside other waiting parents at the school. It was time to pick up our boy. Waiting and waiting, we watched thirty minutes fly by.

Another parent then dashed over to let a group of us know that the bus was stuck in a sand storm. The driver couldn't see the road. An ambulance and a police escort were being sent to lead them out. Some of the children on the bus were having respiratory problems. Of course my husband and I worried. My earlier prayers now made sense, and I said a few more. Two hours later a bus full of dirty teachers and students pulled up to the school. Anxiously we watched and were washed with relief as my stepson exited the bus. He was just fine. He thought the trip had been a great adventure and was eager to tell us all about it.

I don't fully understand why I was fortunate enough to feel the need to pray for my stepson, but I do know God loves his children. If we seek and do the things we know are right, the help is there. Use it.

I know a stepdad that prays for all of his children and

stepchildren, by name, morning and night. He wants all of his children to have the protection of prayer to go with them through their day and through the night.

Our Father in Heaven loves all of His children. Like the stepmother I mentioned earlier, there are times that loving a stepchild feels about as natural as having three armpits. We have to work at it and bite our tongues. Even when we don't feel the warm fuzzies of stepparenthood, our loving Father is still there. We can and need to pray for our stepchildren because they are our Father's children. We've got to use this stepparenting power tool. Because guess what? We too are our Heavenly Father's children, and we need his help. Let's open our hearts to the quiet peace and assurance that accompanies a prayer of faith.

Some other tools have helped me to feel a certain power of effectiveness as a stepparent. Family home evening is definitely a power tool. Of course, every situation is different. In some situations, family home evening would be near impossible. I understand that. All stepparents have to work with the situation they are given and make the most of it as best they can. I love family home evening because it is a time to sing, pray, learn, and plan together. It puts us all on the same playing field for a little while. When we can share family night, we seem more like a family and less like a group of people that only share a roof. Sometimes family night can accomplish things that I cannot.

We went through an episode of dishonesty with my stepdaughter. My husband and I had tried several ways to help this child desire to be honest and prayed in her behalf. We had tried simple things like removing privileges and serious talks about the importance of honesty. We had even gone to greater extremes by creating a lie that involved the child. We invented a trip that she would get to go on.

With great sadness, we explained that the trip was a lie. She was stunned. It was heartbreaking to watch. We carefully explained that we knew she was hurt and that lies hurt. My husband and I thought she would be cured, but we were wrong. The dishonesty continued.

At the end of my rope, I asked my neighbor friend for advice. She lent me a couple of family home evening lessons on honesty. One night, out of fatigue, I asked my stepdaughter to prepare our family home evening lesson. As she was working to select a lesson, a brick of enlightenment dropped on my head. I had her teach one of the lessons on honesty. That little lesson did more to teach the importance of honesty than anything else we'd tried. What a pity we didn't think of it sooner.

Family night also provides us with a venue to accomplish family planning. Planning together, in and of itself, feels like a power tool to me. Finding out what everyone has going on for the week has proven helpful many times. There are still surprises, and I find that the schedule needs to maintain a level of elasticity, but things sure seem to run smoother when I know what's coming.

For example, band concerts used to rattle our little world. On several occasions, I would receive a frantic telephone call at work. A panicked voice on the line would explain that there was a band concert in fifteen minutes. Racing home, I would frantically load up and get everyone on the road for the concert. We'd arrive at the school in a whirlwind and finally catch our breath about the time the concert was ending. We needed a better way to keep track of things. I bought a cheap little weekly planner. During family home evening—after the song and prayer—we take a minute for family business. Each person gives a quick summary of what they have going on during the week. I jot some notes in the planner. Now if we miss something or arrive in a whirlwind, it's not because we didn't plan. It's just because life is a roller coaster ride.

Scouts, music lessons, Church activities, and school activities can act as power tools too. These are all things that I feel have a positive impact in my stepchildren's lives. When I can show my support with the uplifting things that they enjoy, I feel my relationship with them becomes more powerful and better guarded when hard times fall. I cheer at music recitals. I help with school projects. I am a taxi service for scouts and other activities.

When my oldest stepson was working on his Eagle Scout project, I helped him organize a fund-raiser for his project. We worked together to put on a bake sale. We involved the ward and made dozens of phone calls together. We asked volunteers to donate baked goods for the sale. Many hours were invested, and the payoff was a successful bake sale. The community came out to support this boy and his scouting endeavors. It was wonderful to see so many people supporting him. The best part was that when it was all over, my stepson offered me sincere thanks for my help.

Whatever the activity, if it is something positive and uplifting, something that makes the child feel good about himself, it is a power tool. As in the words of the thirteenth Article of Faith: "If there is anything virtuous, lovely, or of good report, or praiseworthy, we seek after these things." We seek after these things for our stepchildren and ourselves. We add power to our relationship as we show our support in things that matter to them. We add power to our relationship as we help to empower them with good experiences and life skills.

Keep a stash of power tools in your stepparenting tool box.

Thirteen

A Man of Faith

To be happy at home is the ultimate result of all ambition.

—Samuel Johnson

In the meridian of time a humble man, a worthy and appointed man, became a stepfather. His name was Joseph, and Jesus Christ was his stepson. With angelic assistance, Joseph willingly took on all the responsibilities of being Christ's earthly father. Joseph taught Jesus the trade that he knew. They were carpenters, humble and faithful. Little is told of the relationship they shared. Little is told of Christ growing up, but there is one particular story I love.

When Jesus was twelve years old, Mary and Joseph took him to Jerusalem, after the custom of the feast. When the festivities were over, they departed and made a full day's journey away from Jerusalem before they realized Jesus was not with them. Turning back to go and find him, they lost over a day's worth of travel, and I'm sure they were out of their minds with worry. Finally, after three days, they found him. He was preaching in the temple.

This story is meaningful in so many ways. At this point, I want look at the role of Joseph. I know I have said that there are things better left to the biological parent, but the influence of a stepparent shouldn't be underestimated. When Christ was missing, Joseph didn't turn to Mary and say, "He's your son. You go find him." They were a team, united. In Luke 2:48 we read, "And when they saw him they were amazed: and his mother said unto him, Son, why hast thou thus dealt with us? Behold thy father and I have sought thee sorrowing."

There was obvious labor involved on the part of both parents in locating their son. Joseph, even as a stepparent, was involved in the rearing of his son. They both sorrowed at his absence and both were amazed when he was found. Was this a twist in Joseph's track? I can only imagine the level of anxiety that he must have felt. To care for another person's child is a great responsibility. For Joseph the task was truly great.

All of us have people who come to our aid. There are many stories of people helping people. We all have opportunities to save someone because our fellow men can be saved on many levels. Sometimes the saving that takes place is urgent, like the time my mother helped a lost child get back to her family. Other times it is a quiet, day-to-day saving, like when my neighbor saw us shoveling rock in our yard. He ignored the rain, grabbed his shovel, and helped us out. We can save others from loneliness, boredom, and fear. Stepparents have a unique obligation to their stepchildren. An admired friend once told me, "You are their (meaning my stepfamily's) salvation." The prospect still keeps me humbled. This friend was referring to the power of a stepparent's example, faith, and love.

My stepmom married my dad when I was already an adult. She could have easily told my dad, "They're your kids, not mine." She did not, and her good influence has been evident in our family for years now. One incident stands out in my mind. During my college years, I dabbled in songwriting and performing. I had my eye on a set of bongo drums in the pawnshop window. Being in college, I was flat broke. It made no sense for me to invest needed money on a little set of drums. My stepmom was aware of my wish for the drums, and she surprised me by buying them for me. I was touched by her thoughtfulness. Now we live in different states, but just knowing she is there and supporting me is a great comfort. The comfort I feel from her is a reminder to me of a stepparent's influence. Our influence can be deep and far reaching.

Stepparenting is a roller coaster ride, and the ride goes on and on. We can take from the example of Joseph, and my good stepparents, the value that we can have in our stepchildren's lives. If we are doing all we can to live a righteous life and to raise a righteous family, we are of tremendous worth in the lives of the children we serve. Faith, patience, and unity in marriage are tools we can take along with us to make this journey a little more pleasant. My journey is not complete, and neither is yours.

Fourteen
Finish the Ride

I have fought a good fight, I have finished my course, I have kept the faith.

—2 Timothy 4:7

Ballroom dancers are very graceful as they twirl across the floor. I wanted to be as graceful and beautiful as they are. When an opportunity arrived to try out for the college ballroom dance team, I jumped at it. Wearing my comfy jeans and a sweater, I went to try out. I met other dancers in leotards, tights, swirling skirts, and high-heeled dance shoes and felt a little out of place. But I wore a number on my back along with the rest of them. The tryout began and the contestants moved effortlessly thought the dances. I moved along with the music like a stumbling child just learning to walk. The dances became progressively more challenging. I bumbled along, willing myself to hang in there. The end result would be worth it.

All the other contestants were moving fluidly across the floor. There were a large number of contestants, and they began to pair up. I was left without a partner. It was clear to me that all of these other dancers had a great deal of experience and were very skilled. I made a conscious choice to bow out of the tryout. I peeled my contestant number off and slipped out. With my limited dance training, I wasn't ready to jump into the big time.

Stepparenting pushes us right into the "big time." We make the team without training or experience. Unlike my tryout, we can't simply pull a number off our backs and walk out. We have a much bigger prize at stake than looking pretty on the dance floor.

We choose our friends, love our children, and try to figure out our stepchildren. We begin with obligatory caring. We care because it is the decent thing to do. We strive to build relationships of trust and mutual respect. We brave the odds and statistics of failure. We give much and train ourselves to expect nothing in return. Each day is taken and lived at face value. When the unexpected happens, for good or for worse, we take it and give it the attention it needs or deserves. We do this because we are the good stepparents. We are the ones who would have let Cinderella keep her bedroom and taken her on family outings. We would have invited the prince over for game night and popcorn.

I have never participated in a marathon. My stamina has not been built up for a long-distance run. Each year, in the newspaper, a list of all the local marathon runners is printed. Along with the runners' names, their completion time is noted. My heart swells with admiration for the individuals who have sacrificed time and energy to train for and complete such a race. Though I have never run, I have spoken with others who have. They tell me that a marathon isn't so much about winning as it is about completion. There is victory and a sense of satisfaction in being able to cross that finish line—to endure to the end.

The race, or ride, of a stepparent is not unlike a marathon. It is a test of endurance. I have felt myself tried and stretched in ways I could not have imagined. Just like stones breaking when water seeps into a fine crack and then freezes, a stepparent can feel like they are cracking under stress and pressure. Every bend and twist in the track is a new adventure. We write our own instruction book or training manual as we try and try again to be good examples and good parents to our stepchildren. As we expect little and give much, with prayer and an honest and pure heart, we are patterning our lives after the Savior's. Striving to live a Christlike life will help us over the turbulent sections of the stepparenting track. Hang in there! You'll make it.

Looking at all of the stories and experiences of other stepparents, I am impressed with the endurance of stepparents. The stepmother I mentioned earlier, the one with the tough stepdaughter, illustrates the value in finishing the ride. A stinky relationship blossomed into something good. Too often stumbling blocks are tossed in a stepparent's way. They entice us to give in, to quit, but what would we be missing if we did? We'd probably miss some heartburn and stress. We'd probably miss out on some tears and regret. But we'd also miss a shot at beautiful friendships with our stepchildren. I have to believe it's worth the ride.

Parents don't parent alone, and stepparents shouldn't try to either. The resources of grandparents, friends, neighbors, teachers, and other extended family members can be a helping hand and a blessing. When I start to feel "wicked," reaching out to one of these individuals can boost my morale. There have been several times when a phone call or visit to one of these people has helped me endure the ride. Initially I was too proud to ask for outside help or recognize it when it was offered. Now, however, I seek the help when I feel it will be beneficial. For example, one morning my stepchildren were reluctant to face the day. They wanted to sit in their beds and watch the grass grow. It was such a beautiful day, and I hated to see them waste it. I let them linger in their beds a long time, and then I called their grandpa. He has a small ranch and often needs help. I asked if he needed help and explained my concerns about the children staying in bed. He then asked to speak with the oldest and asked the boy if he and his siblings would come over and help. My oldest agreed. I did a little victory dance. I didn't have to nag, pester, or bribe the young people out of their beds. Grandpa made it happen. I delivered them to him, and we both had a little chuckle. The kids had a productive day.

As the ride of stepparenting progresses through the years, the track shifts and changes its course. Relationships shift and change. We change too. Life is short. In a blink, it can be gone. The ride we make today is the one that counts the most. Hang onto your harness and be the best stepparent you can be.

Even "wicked" stepparents are God's children. May we be happy and put our endeavors toward returning to live with him. May we each center our life on Christ, press forward, and finish the ride. We'll rewrite the storybooks together with new tales of not-so-wicked stepparents!

Nuggets

Decide what you want to be—pay the price and be what you want to be.

—John A. Widtsoe

Here is a summary of the stepparenthood gems that I have gathered along the way.

- Stay in love. It's why you got into this in the first place.
- Leave to the parent what needs to be left to them as much as you can.
- Stumbling happens. Beverly Sills put it wisely when she said, "You may be disappointed if you fail, but you are doomed if you don't try."
- Time will pass.
- Silence can be priceless.
- Success is in the quiet moments.
- Stepdads can be cool too.

- Character is built one choice and experience at a time.
- A little incentive goes a long way.
- You are a child of God. Remember that, and pray often.
- You don't have to stepparent alone. Use the valuable resources of friends and family for guidance and support.
- Keep the things that really matter in your heart. Remember happiness and laughter.
- Look for the good, take a walk, breathe deep, and hang in there.

About the Author

Sherrie Houston Mackelprang became acquainted with stepparenting as a teenager—giving her stepparents a run for their money. Upon marrying her husband, the tables turned as she became a stepmother to three children. She is a fifth grade teacher and has been working in public education for several years.

0 26575 53016 2